D1173063

DELANEY
STREET
PRESS

Wisdom from
The Garden

Wisdom from
The Garden

*Compiled and Edited
by Criswell Freeman*

DELANEY STREET PRESS
Nashville, TN: 1-800-256-8584

ISBN: 1-58334-069-6

The ideas expressed in this book are not, in all cases, exact quotations, as some have been edited for clarity and brevity. In all cases, the author has attempted to maintain the speaker's original intent. In some cases, material for this book was obtained from secondary sources, primarily print media. While every effort was made to ensure the accuracy of these sources, the accuracy cannot be guaranteed. For additions, deletions, corrections or clarifications in future editions of this text, please write DELANEY STREET PRESS.

Printed in the United States of America
Cover Design by Bart Dawson
Typesetting & Page Layout by Sue Gerdes

2 3 4 5 6 7 8 9 10 • 00 01 02 03 04 05 06

ACKNOWLEDGMENTS

The author gratefully acknowledges the support of Angela Beasley Freeman, Dick and Mary Freeman, Mary Susan Freeman, Jim Gallery, and the team of helpful professionals at Walnut Grove Press and Delaney Street Press.

For Nanny and Her Green Thumb

Table of Contents

Introduction

This little book of quotations celebrates the joys and insights of gardening. In their own words, gardeners, philosophers, poets, and naturalists explore the pleasures of working in the soil.

These quotations remind us that success in the garden depends upon our adherence to certain unchanging principles. The principles on these pages apply to all: veteran gardeners and rank amateurs alike. These ideas, if taken to heart, will enhance not only our gardens, but our lives.

The Author

The Joys
Of Gardening

In a garden, the beauty of God's handiwork is revealed every day. As Mother Nature and Father Time join hands to create their glorious bounty, observant gardeners rejoice.

Whether a three-acre farm or a downtown window-box, a garden is a miraculous place — and hopefully, a joyful one.

What is
paradise?
A garden.

William Lawson

No occupation is so delightful as the culture of the earth.

Thomas Jefferson

Love of gardening is a seed that
once sown never dies.

Gertrude Jekyll

Man is happy in a garden
because God has made him so, and
to live in a garden is the nearest he
can reach to paradise on earth.

Nan Fairbrother

In a thousand unseen ways,
we have drawn shape and strength
from the land.

Lyndon B. Johnson

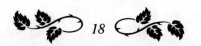

I find the love of a garden grows
upon me more and more
as I grow older.

Maria Edgeworth

I look upon the pleasure which
we take in a garden as one of the
most innocent delights
in human life.

Cicero

One should learn also to enjoy
the neighbor's garden,
no matter how small.

Henry Van Dyke

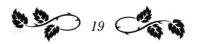

Who loves a garden still
his Eden keeps.

Bronson Alcott

In the beginning God created
the heavens and the earth ...
God saw all that He had made,
and it was very good.

Genesis 1: 1, 31

God almighty first planted
a garden. And, indeed, it is the
purest of human pleasures.

Francis Bacon

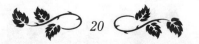

One is nearer God's
heart in a garden
than anywhere else
on earth.

Dorothy Frances Gurney

Gardening has compensations out
of all proportion to its goals.
It is creation in the pure sense.

Phyllis McGinley

What I enjoy is not the fruits alone,
but I also enjoy the soil itself.

Cicero

There is nothing pleasanter than
spading when the ground is
soft and damp.

John Steinbeck

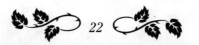

The garden is a
love song,
a duet between a
human being and
Mother Nature.

Jeff Cox

If you want to be happy for an hour, have a party. If you want to be happy for a week, kill your pig and eat it. But if you want to be happy all your life, become a gardener.

Chinese Saying

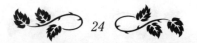

He who plants a garden
    plants happiness.

Chinese Proverb

Live now, believe me,
    wait not till tomorrow;
gather the roses of life today.

Pierre de Ronsard

Happiness is a habit. Cultivate it.

Elbert Hubbard

The gardening bug can bite
at any moment.

Barbara Damrosch

Gardening is a kind of self-prescribed
preventative medicine,
good for all ills.

Sheryl London

To own a bit of ground, to scratch it
with a hoe, to plant seeds, and
watch their renewal of life —
this is the commonest
delight of the race, the
most satisfactory thing
a man can do.

Charles Dudley Warner

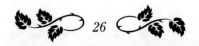

The man who has
planted a garden
feels that he
has done
something for
the good of
the whole world.

Charles Dudley Warner

You're only here
for a short visit.
Stop to smell
the flowers
along the way.

Walter Hagen

The Laws
Of the Harvest

Mother Nature conducts her affairs according to a strict set of rules. Wise gardeners follow those rules and reap a lifetime of happy harvests. But woe to the slothful gardener who seeks to cut corners: Mother Nature does not reward those who seek to circumvent her laws.

As planting season approaches, remember Mother Nature's unwavering law of the harvest: Over the long run, you will reap as you sow... in the garden and in life.

To have the harvest
    we must sow the seed.

             Liberty Hyde Bailey

As you plan your garden,
    consider the element of time.
The flowers that bloom in May
will not be blooming in August.

             Barbara Damrosch

Nature goes her own way,
    and all that to us seems an
      exception is really
      according to order.

             Goethe

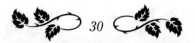

Nature, to be commanded, must be obeyed.

Francis Bacon

Man masters nature
    not by force but by
      understanding.
Jacob Bronowski

The first rule of successful
    gardening is to work with,
not against, the natural setting.
Burpee Complete Gardener

Climate is the single-most
    important factor in how plants
grow — indeed in what we select
    to plant in the first place.
Jack Kramer

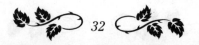

32

The wise
gardener
anticipates
June in
January.

House and Garden

The farmer who takes everything from the land without restitution will become the servant of wiser men, either on the farm or elsewhere.

C. E. Thorne

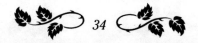

Whatsoever a man
soweth, that shall
he also reap.

Galatians 6:7

Nature soon takes over if the gardener is absent.

Penelope Hobhouse

A gardener is the spirit
of the garden, the organizing force,
the heart and soul of it all.

Jeff Cox

Deciding what to grow is
one of the most enjoyable
aspects of gardening.

Burpee Complete Gardener

Show me your garden
and I shall tell you
what you are.

Alfred Austin

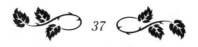

Did you ever think how a bit
of land displays the character
of the owner?

Laura Ingalls Wilder

I guess a good gardener starts
as a good weeder.

Amos Pettingill

Pray for a good
harvest, but
continue
to hoe.

Old Saying

The spontaneous
energies of the earth
are a gift of nature,
but they require
the labors of man
to direct their
operation.

Thomas Jefferson

Working the Soil

Those who work the soil are blessed. Few experiences in life can match the satisfaction gained from quietly sinking a spade into God's rich, dark earth.

The soil, properly tended, becomes the canvas upon which the gardener creates his or her artwork. If you wish to make *your* plot of ground a timeless work of art, consider the following ideas.

Working in the garden
gives me something
beyond the enjoyment
of the senses. It gives me
a profound feeling
of inner peace.

Ruth Stout

What this country needs
is dirtier fingernails
and cleaner minds.

Will Rogers

The greatest gift of a garden
is the restoration of the
five senses.

Hanna Rion

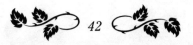

Put in the plow
and plant the
great hereafter
in the now.

Robert Browning

There is a common error
of thought that all virgin soils
are necessarily good.
Nature laid down her soil
in a haphazard way.

Louis Bromfield

Babylon died because
its soil died.

The Nashville Tennessean

Every gardener knows
　　that one of the chief joys
of his activity is working deeply
　　with the soil, pushing
one's hands deep into its moist,
　　life-giving crumbliness.

Jeff Cox

First prepare a deep,
　　loose seedbed,
　　and then don't walk on it.

Dick Raymond

My good hoe, as it bites the ground,
    revenges my wrongs, and I have
      less lust to bite my enemies.
    In smoothing the rough hillocks,
      I smooth my temper.

Ralph Waldo Emerson

What is it about gardening
    that works out something bad?

Anne Chotzinoff Grossman

We have no time to sin
    when we devote our time
      to working in the garden
        with God.

Jim G. Brown

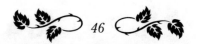

From labor comes health;
from health, contentment springs.

James Beattie

After the fine exercise
in the garden, I have an appetite
like a 12-year-old and have
no sleepless nights.

Jim G. Brown

The highest reward for
man's toil is not what
he gets for it but what
he becomes by it.

John Ruskin

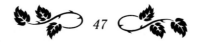 47

No garden is without weeds.
Thomas Fuller

Weed your own garden first.
Old Saying

A man's best friends are
his ten fingers.
Robert Collyear

In order to live
off the garden,
you practically
have to live
in it.

Kin Hubbard

Plough deep while
sluggards sleep;
and you shall have
corn to sell
and to keep.

Ben Franklin

All work is as seed sown; it grows
and spreads, and sows itself anew.
Thomas Carlyle

Those who labor in the earth
are the chosen people of God.
Thomas Jefferson

Though the wide universe is
full of good, no kernel of nourishing
corn can come to him but through his
toil bestowed on that plot of ground
which is given to him to till.
Ralph Waldo Emerson

We are here to cultivate
the garden and take care of it.
Genesis 2:15

He who would eat the fruit
must climb the tree.
Scottish Proverb

Gardens are not made by singing,
"Oh, how beautiful," and sitting
in the shade.
Rudyard Kipling

All gardens are
a form of autobiography.

Robert Dash

As is the gardener,
so is the garden.

Old Saying

You cannot plough a field
by turning it over
in your mind.

Old Saying

 53

A garden
is a thing of
beauty and a
job forever.

Richard Briers

Hope for the Harvest

Gardeners are, by nature, optimists. They pour seeds, water, time, and effort into a plot of dirt with absolutely no guarantee of return. Planting a garden is faith in action. More often than not, that faith is rewarded.

On the pages that follow, we examine ways that hope-filled gardeners bring forth their harvests. These experts always hold out great hope for the next big harvest, and hopefully you will too.

Gardeners,
I think, dream
bigger dreams
than emperors.

Mary Cantwell

At the heart of
gardening there
is a belief
in the miraculous.

Mirabel Osler

Take nature's vagaries and pranks in stride.

Ruth Shaw Ernst

Gardening is the best therapy
in the world.

C. Z. Guest

Let us not be weary in
well doing; for in due season we
shall reap, if we faint not.

Galatians 6:9

By trusting in Thee,
we know our labors are not in
vain and that our
harvest is great.

Jim G. Brown's Garden Prayer for 1945

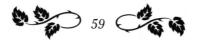

Seeds of discouragement will not grow in a thankful heart.

Anonymous

A Gardener's Education

A gardener's education is never completed. Even the most seasoned veteran has much to learn and so little time in which to learn it.

The following quotations remind us that every garden doubles as a classroom. And for wise gardeners, school is always in session.

Nature is always
hinting at us.

Robert Frost

Listen to Nature's teachings.

William Cullen Bryant

Man is wise and constantly in quest
of more wisdom; but the ultimate
wisdom, which deals with beginnings,
remains locked in a seed.

Hal Borland

Nature's lessons will remain
opaque as long as we are full
of our own ideas and preconceptions.

Jeff Cox

True wisdom consists in not
departing from nature but
in molding our conduct according
to her laws and models.

Marcus Annaeus Seneca

There is no other door
to knowledge than the door
Nature opens.

Luther Burbank

Nature's instructions are
always slow; those of men
are generally premature.

Rousseau

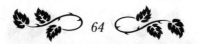

Study nature as the
countenance of God.

Charles Kingsley

It is the marriage of the
soul with Nature that makes
the intellect fruitful
and gives birth
to imagination.

Henry David Thoreau

A modest garden contains, for those who know how to look and to wait, more instruction than a library.

Henri Frédéric Amiel

Gardening is an art which
is learned by practice,
experience, and sensible advice.

Jules Oravetz, Sr.

The life so short, the craft
so long to learn. This was said
about literature, but it really fits
gardening better.

Henry Mitchell

The more one gardens,
the more one learns; and the
more one learns, the more one
realizes how little one knows.
I suppose the whole of life
is like that.

V. Sackville-West

To him who in the love
of nature holds communion with
her visible forms, she speaks
a various language.

William Cullen Bryant

The love of flowers
is really the best
teacher of how
to grow and
understand them.

Max Schling

Give me a spark of Nature's fire. That's all the learning I desire.

Robert Burns

Patience

Mother Nature moves at her own pace and will not be hurried. Even the most impatient gardener cannot speed the harvest. Thus gardening is, and forever will be, an exercise in patience.

Savvy gardeners are patient gardeners, as the following quotations will attest.

Sweet flowers are
slow and weeds
make haste.

William Shakespeare

Patience is power;
with time and
patience the
mulberry leaf
becomes silk.

Chinese Proverb

Patience

P atience is a bitter plant,
      but it has sweet fruit.

German Proverb

I f you enjoy fruit,
      pluck not the flower.

Old Saying

W ith plants, persuasion
      is better than force.

Elsa Bakalar

There is more to life
    than increasing its speed.
Gandhi

Teach us, O Lord, the
    disciplines of patience,
    for we find that to wait is
    often harder than to work.
Peter Marshall

Patience and diligence, like faith,
    move mountains.
William Penn

Basic to an integrated life is a dominant ideal. To plow a straight row one must keep his eye on the goal rather than the plow.

J. M. Price

Adopt the pace
of nature; her
secret is
patience.

Ralph Waldo Emerson

Bring forth fruit with patience.

Luke 8:15

Reverence

God first met man in a garden, and He continues to do so. A well-tended garden can be a holy place. It can be a place for quiet contemplation and spiritual renewal.

Perhaps, then, we should approach the garden as we would enter a church: with respect and awe. After all, God first met man in a garden, and that little plot of dirt can still become a sanctuary to those who approach it with reverence.

Nature is the
living, visible
garment of
God.

Goethe

All of God's earth is holy ground.

Joaquin Miller

Reverence

Adam was a gardener,
and God who made him sees,
That half a proper
gardener's work,
is done upon his knees.

Rudyard Kipling

Look through nature
up to nature's God.

Alexander Pope

He who plants a garden works
hand-in-hand with God.

Malloch

Gardening is an instrument
of grace.

May Sarton

A gardener's relationship
with the soil is little short of
a religious experience.

Bernard Schofield

The word "miracle"
aptly describes a seed.

Jack Kramer

Flowers are sunshine, food, and medicine to the soul.

Luther Burbank

The soil is a wonderful thing.
Treat it like a good old friend.

Fred Streeter

Touch the earth,
love the earth,
honour the earth.

Henry Beston

Confronted with the vision
of a beautiful garden, we see
something beautiful about
ourselves, as a part of nature.

Jeff Cox

Into every empty corner,
into all forgotten things and nooks,
Nature struggles to pour life,
pouring life into the dead,
life into life itself.

Henry Beston

Let all the earth fear the Lord;
let all the inhabitants of the world
stand in awe of him.

Psalm 33:8

The entire earth is a garden,
a natural garden.

Jamie Jobb

What nature delivers to us
is never stale, because what nature
creates has eternity in it.

Isaac Bashevis Singer

God, I can push the grass apart
And lay my finger on Thy heart!

Edna St. Vincent Millay

The only words that ever
satisfied me as describing Nature
are the terms used in fairy books:
"charm," "spell," "enchantment."

G. K. Chesterton

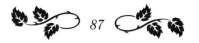

Nothing in all creation is so like God as stillness.

Meister Eckhart

The Grateful Gardener

Thoughtful gardeners are thankful gardeners. The blessings and bounties of a carefully tended patch of dirt are almost impossible to ignore, especially for seasoned veterans.

Every moment spent working in the soil is a special gift for those wise enough to appreciate their good fortune. So if you're lucky enough to be a gardener, be a grateful gardener. You'll discover that happiness is the greatest harvest of all.

See Nature,
and through her,
God.

Henry David Thoreau

Flowers are heaven's masterpieces.

Dorothy Parker

One of the most
delightful things
about a garden is
the anticipation
it provides.

W. E. Johns

Deviation from Nature
is deviation from happiness.

Samuel Johnson

Happiness is a wayside flower
growing upon the highways
of usefulness.

Anonymous

One touch of nature
makes the whole world kin.

William Shakespeare

Beauty is God's handwriting.
Welcome it in every fair face,
every fair sky, every fair flower.

Charles Kingsley

One of the most important
things a gardener does is *look*.
The rewards are immeasurable.

Elsa Bakalar

Nature is painting for us,
day after day, pictures of
infinite beauty if only we have
the eyes to see them.

John Ruskin

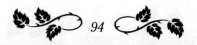

Never lose an opportunity of seeing anything that is beautiful, for beauty is God's handwriting — a wayside sacrament.

Ralph Waldo Emerson

Nature will bear the closest inspection. She invites us to lay our eye level with her smallest leaf, and take an insect's view of its plain.

Henry David Thoreau

The only thing different
about having a green thumb is that
you don't get discouraged by
failure. When something doesn't
work, you try again.

Beth Weidner

Nature and the garden
bring out the best in
our characters.

Felicity Bryan

True joy is serene.

Marcus Annaeus Seneca

Flowers and plants are
silent presences; they nourish
every sense but the ear.

May Sarton

Flowers are our
greatest silent friends.

Jim G. Brown

Silence is but a rich pause
in the music of life.

Sarojini Naidu

The Grateful Gardener

To create a little flower is
the labour of ages.
William Blake

Flowers may beckon us,
but they speak toward
heaven and God.
Henry Ward Beecher

Flowers are the sweetest things
God ever made and forgot to put
a soul into.
Henry Ward Beecher

Wisdom from
The Garden

We conclude with a potpourri of helpful hints and thought-provoking observations designed to make your thumb green and your heart light.

May all your harvests be bountiful, and may all your gardening experiences be joyful.

Good gardening
is very simple,
really. You just
have to think like
a plant.

Barbara Damrosch

Too often gardeners start with seed
instead of graph paper.

Helen Van Pelt Wilson

Planning a garden on paper
is simple — but important.

Jamie Jobb

Nature does not complete things.
She is chaotic. Man must finish, and
he does so by making a garden and
building a wall.

Robert Frost

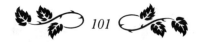 *101*

Creating a garden is like making music: The least distraction is apt to destroy the melodic line.

Beverly Nichols

The early morning has gold in its mouth.

Ben Franklin

Never give up listening to the sounds of birds.

John James Audubon

We need the tonic of the wilderness.

Henry David Thoreau

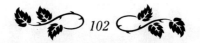

The amen of
Nature
is always
a flower.

Oliver Wendell Holmes

One of the most soothing
sounds of nature is the laughter
of falling water.

Jeff Cox

The most sublime state a human
being can aspire to is being
in the wilderness alone
with God.

Malcolm Muggeridge

I love to be alone. I never found
the companion that was
so companionable
as solitude.

Henry David Thoreau

If a tree dies,
plant
another in
its place.

Linnaeus

No place on earth is more
    sensuous than a garden.

Jeff Cox

Most people don't see the sun,
soil, bugs, seeds, plants, moon, water,
    clouds, and wind the way
        gardeners do.

Jamie Jobb

We do not see nature with
our eyes, but with our understanding
        and our hearts.

William Hazlitt

When I first open
my eyes upon
the morning
meadows and look
out upon the
beautiful world,
I thank God
I am alive.

Ralph Waldo Emerson

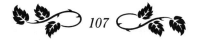

Growing a garden and staying out
in the fresh air after office hours
seemed to give me the strength
to meet all problems
with greater courage.

Jim G. Brown

In my garden, care stops at
the gate and gazes at me wistfully
through the bars.

Alexander Smith

All my hurts my
garden spade can heal.

Ralph Waldo Emerson

There is something about sun and soil that heals broken bodies and jangled nerves.

Nature Magazine

Although much of the
pleasure in gardening derives
from serendipitous effects,
thorough planning is essential.

Tom Wright

The plans of the diligent
lead to profit.

Proverbs 21:5

Think about the garden as
a small community of plants and
animals coexisting with one
another and with human beings.

Ruth Shaw Ernst

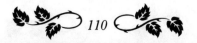

Well-balanced gardens
have a quality of restfulness and
exquisite perfection, with plants
chosen and placed like words
in a perfect poem.

Jeff Cox

The essence of the enjoyment
of a garden is that things should
look as though they like
to grow in it.

Beatrix Farrand

We think birds are valuable and keep three birdbaths on our front and side lawns. The birds no doubt destroy many of the harmful insects.

Jim G. Brown

Fortunately for man, the insect world is divided against itself. Far more than half the insects prey upon other insects.

Edwin Way Teale

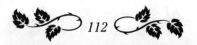

The trouble with garden bugs is simple. People don't know enough about them. Most bugs in your garden are good for the garden. Get to know them.

Jamie Jobb

As you learn more about gardening, every new experience means more to you and makes a long-lasting impression.

Rosemary Verey

Little flower — but if I could understand what you are, root and all; then, all in all, I should know what God and man is.

Alfred, Lord Tennyson

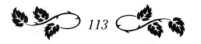

If you garden, you think about gardens. Ideas keep manifesting themselves; they seep into your mind often when you are nowhere near a garden.

Mirabel Osler

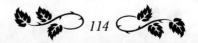

Man must go back to nature for information.

Thomas Paine

A garden is a link to
the passing seasons.

Sheryl London

Here is the great mystery
of life and growth: Everything is
changing, growing, aiming at
something, but silently, unboastfully,
taking its time.

Ruth Stout

Things seem to move very slowly
in a garden. But nothing ever
remains the same.

Jamie Jobb

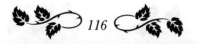

Nature gives to every time
and season some beauties
of its own.

Charles Dickens

Every gardener knows under
the cloak of winter lies a miracle:
a seed waiting to sprout....
And the anticipation nurtures
our dreams.

Barbara Winkler

Come to the garden,
The soul's sweet bouquet
The flowers of tomorrow
Are in the seeds of today.

JoAnna O'Keefe

Day's sweetest moments
        are at dawn.
                Ella Wheeler Wilcox

How fair is a garden amid
        the toils and passions
                of existence.
                Benjamin Disraeli

I should like to enjoy this summer
        flower by flower,
                as if it were to be
                the last one for me.
                        André Gide

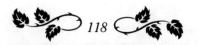

There are two seasonal
diversions that can ease the
bite of any winter. One is the
January thaw. The other is
the seed catalogues.

Hal Borland

Though nothing can bring
back the hour
Of splendor in the grass,
of glory in the flower;
We will grieve not, rather find
Strength in what
remains behind.

William Wordsworth

No winter lasts forever,
  no spring skips its turn.
   April is a promise that May
is bound to keep, and we know it.

Hal Borland

Gardening really has no beginning
and no end. In particular, pleasures
  of the sense of smell really
     know no seasons.

Tovah Martin

No matter what changes take place
    in the world, or in me,
  nothing ever seems to disturb
     the face of spring.

E. B. White

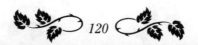

Each day is born
anew for him
who takes
it rightly.

James Russell Lowell

Bloom where
you're planted.

Mary Engelbreit

Sources

Sources

Alcott, Bronson 20
Amiel, Frédéric, Henri 66
Audubon, John James 102
Austin, Alfred 37
Bacon, Francis 20, 31
Bailey, Liberty Hyde 30
Bakalar, Elsa 74, 94
Beattie, James 47
Beecher, Henry Ward 98
Beston, Henry 85, 86
Blake, William 98
Borland, Hal 63, 119, 120
Briers, Richard 54
Bromfield, Louis 44
Bronowski, Jacob 32
Brown, Jim G. 46, 47, 59, 97, 108, 112
Browning, Robert 43
Bryan, Felicity 96
Bryant, William Cullen 63, 68
Burbank, Luther 64, 84
Burns, Robert 70
Burpee Complete Gardener 32, 37
Cantwell, Mary 56
Carlyle, Thomas 51
Chesterton, G. K. 87
Cicero 19, 22
Collyear, Robert 48
Cox, Jeff 23, 37, 45, 63, 85, 104, 106, 111
Damrosch, Barbara 26, 30, 100
Dash, Robert 53
de Ronsard, Pierre 25

Sources

Wisdom from the Garden

About the Author

Criswell Freeman is a Doctor of Clinical Psychology living in Nashville, Tennessee. He is the author of *When Life Throws You a Curveball, Hit It* and *The Wisdom Series* from WALNUT GROVE PRESS. He is also the author of numerous quotation books published by DELANEY STREET PRESS.

About
DELANEY STREET PRESS

DELANEY STREET PRESS publishes books designed to inspire and entertain readers of all ages. DELANEY STREET books are distributed by Walnut Grove Press. For more information, call 1-800-256-8584.